40 SCRIPTURE BASED PRAYERS TO PRAY OVER YOUR WIFE

KAYLENE YODER

Copyright ©2017 Kaylene Yoder

www.kayleneyoder.com

Published by HumbleWise Press

All rights reserved. No part of this publication may be reproduced or transmitted in any form or by any means, electronic or mechanical, including photocopying, recording, or by any information storage or retrieval system without the written permission of the author. The only exception being for brief quotations in printed reviews which include full reference to the book and author. When reviewing online the author's name and website, www.kayleneyoder.com, must be included.

ISBN: 978-0-9996380-2-6 (print), 978-0-9996380-3-3 (epub)

Unless otherwise indicated, Scripture references are taken from the HOLY BIBLE, NEW INTERNATIONAL VERSION®. Copyright ©1973, 1978, 1984 by International Bible Society.
Used by permission of Zondervan.
All rights reserved.

Scripture quotations marked KJV are taken from the HOLY BIBLE, KING JAMES VERSION®. Copyright ©1977, 1984, 2001 by Thomas Nelson, Inc. Used by permission. All rights reserved.

Publishing and Design Services | MartinPublishingServices.com

Stock Photography: 123rf.com
Contributors: alga38, anamomarques, anskuw, azalia, belchonock, chris_elwell, egal, erostunova, karandaev, kellyplz, kuzmichstudio, loonara, lyulka12, mashe, neirfy, pat138241, photoauris, photoncatcher, prakobkit, saddako, serazetdinov, sinseeho, stephaniefrey, steve_byland, szefei, Taiga, teerawit, tepikina, tomnamon, tuvi, valery_potapova, varts, vladir09, wollertz, yasonya,

CONTENTS

Introduction / 1

Praying for You, Her Husband / 5
Protecting Your Marriage / 9
Preparing for Your Marriage Bed / 11
Guarding Her Eyes / 13
Guarding Her Mind / 15
A Right Heart / 17
A Greater Faith / 19
A Better Attitude / 21
Her Love for Others / 23
Finding Joy in Trials / 25
Claiming Peace / 27
Growing in Patience / 29
Practicing Kindness / 31
Becoming Good / 33
Her Faithfulness / 35
Practicing Self-control / 37
Seeking Wisdom / 39
Developing Integrity / 41
Keeping Honest / 43
Humility: A Way of Life / 45
Courage for the Way / 49
Repentance and Forgiving Others / 51
Trusting God for His Promises / 53
Hearing the Lord / 55

Contents

Obedience When Called / 57
Her Submissive Leadership / 59
Purposeful Motherhood / 61
Her Work and Gifts / 65
Confidence in Her Callings / 69
Protection for the Day / 71
A Worthy Example / 73
The Paths She Walks / 75
The Words She Speaks / 79
Covering Her Choices / 81
Evaluating Friendships / 83
Health of Body and Soul / 85
Healthy Emotions / 87
Overcoming Habits / 89
Victory Over Her Past / 91
Hope for the Future / 95

ABCs of Christian Marriage / 97

DEDICATION

For my Sam

Thank you for
every prayer,
your daily hugs,
and each encouraging word.

I love you, always.

INTRODUCTION

Ever since publishing the first few prayers for wives to pray over their husbands at kayleneyoder.com, I've received requests from gentlemen who want prayers they can pray over their wives. I blew it off saying, "I'm not called to write for men, but you might find that the Scriptures in the prayers are helpful for fashioning your own prayers."

However, the requests kept coming in, and finally I had to acknowledge that about twenty-five percent of the people praying the prayers I've written are my brothers in Christ. Even today they are praying the prayers for their wives simply by tweaking the pronouns into feminine tense as they pray.

That's the beauty of prayers rooted in Scripture – they can be prayed for anyone. This kind of intercession is appropriate for the unborn to the mature, for the married, separated, single, engaged, even for ourselves.

The Bible is living and active, speaking and relevant to all who are willing to hear. God's Word holds healing and power for those who dare speak it out loud, delivering courage to crippled hearts that grasp at the hope He gives.

I don't know why you selected this book of prayers. Perhaps you are praying for your beautiful new bride. Possibly you are bringing your broken marriage before the Lord for supernatural healing. Maybe you are on your last straw and chose this book on a whim, thinking prayer will change your wife.

I thought prayer would fix my husband, too. And it did. But not before God started fixing me.

You see, prayer and Scriptures aren't just some magical tools we get to wave around against someone else in hopes to make our situations better. God's Word and ways are not to be used to push our own agenda or manipulate others into compliance to our will.

I'm convinced God will absolutely fix your wife. However, most likely He will first equip you to be the tool He can use to show Himself to your wife and family. I believe we often hinder our own prayers without realizing it. Psalm 34:15 says, "The eyes of the Lord are on the righteous and His ears are attentive to their cry". And again in verse 17, "The righteous cry out, and the Lord hears them; He delivers them from all their troubles." Apparently, having our own hearts right before the Lord speaks louder than our most eloquent praying efforts.

So, my brother in Christ, I pray you will find hope and healing as you pray for your wife and marriage. May your heart be strengthened and your faith emboldened. And may the Father's peace and joy anoint you daily. Whatever situation you find yourself in, humbly ask the Lord to grow you in Himself first, then trust God to work in your wife.

Your job is to love and pray. It's God's job to do the fixing.

1 Peter 3:7

"Husbands, in the same way
be considerate as you
live with your wives,
and treat them with
respect as the weaker partner
and as heirs with you of the
gracious gift of life,
so that nothing will
hinder your prayers."

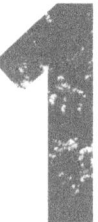

PRAYING FOR YOU, HER HUSBAND

Husbands,
love your wives
and do not be
harsh with them.

Colossians 3:19

Romans 12:9-12
Malachi 2:13-16
Ephesians 4:22-24
Philippians 4:5-7

Father God, thank You for this beautiful woman You have blessed me with. Thank you for how far You have brought us. You have proven to be faithful. You have proven to be present. You have proven to be good, oh, so good. My heart overflows with praise and thanksgiving to You.

Reflecting on our marriage, I am convicted that I haven't always been the husband You have called me to be to my wife. I confess the times I have been disrespectful and unloving in words, attitudes, and deeds. I see them as You do: sin. Lord, remove any bitterness, selfishness, and impatience from my heart. In those places plant ready forgiveness, patience, and the willingness to bear all things (Ephesians 4:2).

Make me kind, Lord. Make me gentle. Teach me Your ways. Transform my heart into a gentle, grace-extending one. Make me faithful, not only in body, but also in the way I speak and behave toward my wife. Make me the kind of husband who will not do or say anything to degrade or devalue my wife. Renew my mind so I can judge my words and actions based on Your truth and not just by how I feel. Work in me to become the man worthy of my wife's trust. Help her know that I aim to bring her good and not evil all the days of my life (Galatians 6:10).

Father, I know my first and foremost duty is to my wife. Remind me of this often throughout the day. Help me seek ways to bless her with my words and actions. When words are inappropriate, guard my tongue, Lord (Psalm 141:3). Help me understand that sometimes my words are wrong, no matter how right I am. Help me discern and choose when to speak and when to remain quiet.

Transform me, Lord. Remind me not to put pressure on my wife to fulfill me in ways only You can. Help me lay all my expectations at Your feet instead of hers. Help me accept my wife the way she is and not try to change her into what I want her to look like, act like, or be. I release her to You to be molded, shaped, and grown into the woman You had in mind when You created her.

Father, work in me daily, that I might become the husband of my wife's dreams, one she can love easily, trust fully, laugh with, cry with, and grow old with. Lord, give my wife a new husband, and let it be me. Oh, Lord, let it be me - completely transformed, fitting perfectly into the plan You have for her life and our marriage. In Jesus' name, Amen.

Trust
Scripture Readings

Psalm 33:13-22

Psalm 32:6-11

Psalm 37:1-9

Psalm 40:1-5

Psalm 44:4-8

Psalm 55:16-23

Isaiah 50:4-10

Isaiah 51:12-16

Psalm 62.1-9

Psalm 84:6-12

2

PROTECTING YOUR MARRIAGE

Unite us, Father.
Preserve and strengthen
our allegiance to
each other and You.

Amen.

Romans 12:3
Romans 14:19
Romans 15:5
1 Corinthians 1:10

Jesus, thank You for the perfect picture of marriage through Your relationship with the church. Help my wife and me replicate that model in ways glorifying to You. Teach us to love one another and "make every effort to do what leads to peace and to mutual edification" (Romans 14:19).

Father, don't let us grow apart or become comfortable in going our own ways, but bring unity between us so that we may be like-minded toward one another (Romans 15:5). Lord, I lift our marriage to You, asking that You refine us to be "perfectly united in mind and thought" (1 Corinthians 1:10).

Lord, I pray our commitment to You and to each other will grow stronger every day, binding together a tie that is not easily broken. Infuse us with the power of love in its purest form. Teach us to be kind to one another, tenderhearted, forgiving one another, just as we are forgiven in Christ (Ephesians 4:32). Let us not grow weary of doing good to each other, so that at just the right time we may reap an abundant harvest (Galatians 6:9).

Lord, I pray You will protect us from anything that could harm or destroy our marriage. When trials persist, bring us out with a stronger marriage and faith. Let nothing come into our hearts, minds, and actions that could threaten our marriage. I take a stand against the enemy's schemes to divide us through the lusts of the eyes and flesh. Open our discernment to recognize bitterness, jealousy, irritation, doubt, distrust or the like, and not let them grow into a full blown division of our marriage.

Father, unite us. Solidify us in You. Give us one mind and one spirit. And make our marriage a blessing to us. May we find fulfillment, meaning, and purpose, ever growing in our commitment to each other. Protect us, Father. Preserve and strengthen our allegiance to each other and You. In Jesus' name, Amen.

PREPARING FOR YOUR MARRIAGE BED

Enjoy life
with your wife,
whom you love...

Ecclesiastes 9:9

Proverbs 5:15-20
Hebrews 13:4
1 Corinthians 7:2-5

Father God, thank you for this beautiful woman You have blessed me with. I pray You would give her an increased sense of fulfillment in our physical time together. Help her see herself as I do, a precious and flawless gift to be treasured and held dear.

Father, You have designed my wife and I with very intimate needs for each others body. Teach me how to give myself gently, yet wholeheartedly. Remind me to take into consideration her needs above mine. Lord, I ask that You would help my wife become confident in sharing her sexual desires with me. Help her not see sex as a chore or duty, but to find fulfillment in our times of physically coming together.

I pray my wife will be understanding toward me, but mostly let me be understanding of her, setting an example of what it means to lay my life down for hers. May we both be satisfied and captivated by each other's love (Proverbs 5:19). May our marriage bed be kept pure and honorable before You. And may we not partake of anything that would defile the purity of our marriage bed. Father, I stand against any temptations of extra-marital affairs or adulterous thoughts. May our trust in each other never be broken or endangered by the schemes of the enemy or evil plans of others.

Father, I pray that You will remove any remembrances or enticements of any other intimate relationships my wife or I may have had prior to our commitment to each other. Purify our minds from any wanderings or longings of past relationships. Keep us excited for each other, growing together in kindness and understanding. Today, Father, renew our rapture for each other and our devotion to each other, so that the enemy will lose any foothold he may have in our hearts and minds. As we continue to become one in the flesh, may we ever bring glory to You, the Author and Creator of intimacy. In Jesus name, Amen.

GUARDING HER EYES

I pray the eyes of
my wife's heart
will be enlightened,
so that she may know
the hope to which
You have called her.

Amen.

Ezekiel 20:7-8
Matthew 6:22-23
Ephesians 1:18-19

Father, we know our eyes are the lamps of our bodies. With them, we introduce either light or darkness into our hearts (Matthew 6:22-23). Give my wife the courage to guard her eyes from any evil. Remove from her any desire to indulge in pornography, crude humor, books, articles or television shows that do not promote purity of heart, mind, and soul. If there is any hidden sin, Lord, convict my wife to seek to rid herself of harmful practices so that she will not defile herself.

Lord, I know You cannot tolerate wrong (Habakkuk 1:13). I believe that You will pour out Your wrath and spend Your anger on those who do not obey Your command to remove any defiling images or idols (Ezekiel 20:7-8) in their lives. Spare my wife from Your anger, and strengthen her to do as You bid in keeping her body, the temple of the Holy Spirit, pure. I pray You will be patient with her, yet persistent in refining her for Your glory.

Jesus, I pray also that the eyes of my wife's heart will be enlightened, so that she may know the hope to which You have called her. Help her know the riches of Your inheritance and Your incomparably great power. May this knowledge further motivate her toward the purity of her eyes, the lamp of her body (Ephesians 1:18-19).

Lord, I ask that you would reveal Yourself to my wife in new ways. Help her see You. Help her find You. Put a desire in her to seek You until she finds You. Do not let her wander as one who is blind. Give her purpose and a vision that points solely toward Your plan for her life. In Jesus' mighty name, Amen.

GUARDING HER MIND

Therefore, prepare
your minds for action;
be self-controlled;
set your hope fully
on the grace to be
given you when
Jesus Christ is revealed.

1 Peter 1:13

Romans 8:5-8
Ephesians 4:22-24
2 Corinthians 2:10
Timothy 1:7

Father God, You know and discern our thoughts and the intents of our hearts (Hebrews 4:12). Do not let my wife walk in ways that are not good, pursuing her own desires and imaginations. Instead, make her wise and discerning, giving her a mind like Christ's (1 Corinthians 2:16). Help her always weigh her thoughts with the truth of Your Word.

Father, we know those who live according to sinful nature have their minds set on what that nature desires (Romans 8:5). We also know that because evil-minded people don't think it worthwhile to retain knowledge of You, You give them over to depraved minds. They become filled with all the wicked, senseless, faithless, heartless, ruthless things they desire (Romans 1:28-31).

Father, I stand in faith, praying You will protect my wife from any thought habits that could result in diseases of the mind. I pray You remove any spirits of fear, negativity, impurity, selfishness, anger, and the like from my wife's mind. Replace such things with a sound mind, one that has the power to think rightly and justly, one that dwells on Your truth.

Lord, I pray my wife will not be conformed to any pattern of this world, but be transformed by the renewing of her mind (Romans 12:2). Help her take captive every thought and making it obedient to You (2 Corinthians 10:5) so that she will be able to test and approve what is your good and perfect will in all circumstances (Romans 12:2).

Lord, I lift my wife to You to be made new in her thoughts. Convict her in any area You would like her to grow or heal from, then enable her to stand against the enemy when an attack is made on her mind. Strengthen her with a clear mind and self control, so she can hear You when she prays (1 Peter 4:7). Help my wife think only on things that are true, noble, right, pure, and lovely - whatever is admirable or praiseworthy - so that the peace of God which, surpasses all understanding, will be able to guard her heart and mind in Christ Jesus (Philippians 4:8,7). In Jesus' name, Amen.

A RIGHT HEART

Teach me Your way,
O Lord, and I will
walk in Your truth;
give me an undivided heart
that I may fear Your name.

Psalm 139:23-24

Proverbs 27:19
Jeremiah 17:9-10
Hebrews 4:12

Father, thank You for giving my wife a heart that is teachable. Even when she is unwilling to change her views or ways I trust You, oh Lord, have the power to work in her heart and make it pliable to Your will and Your ways. Create in her a new and a steadfast spirit (Psalm 51:10) for You have not given my wife a heart of stone but of flesh.

Your Word teaches us a good person brings good things out of the goodness of their heart, and an evil person brings evil things out of their heart (Luke 6:45). Lord, help my wife stand firmly in righteousness that overflows from a heart ablaze for You. Teach her to walk in Your truth. Give her an undivided heart (Psalm 86:11), that has no room to entertain both good and evil. Continue to grow her gentle and wise in heart, centered and settled in You so she may be living proof of Your love and power.

Father, You have said, "I, the Lord, search the heart and examine the mind, to reward a man according to his conduct, according to what his deeds deserve" (Jeremiah 17:9-10). Search my heart, Jesus. And ever so gently, search my wife's heart. Test us both and know our thoughts. See if there is any offensive way in us as a marriage unit and in each of us individually. Convict us in any areas where we need to grow more gentle, humble, kind, loving or repentant, then guide us into Your everlasting way (Psalm 139:23-24).

Lord, when the road gets hard, do not let my wife's heart be troubled. Prove Yourself to her so her trust in You may be established, further purifying her heart by faith. May she come to praise You with all her heart, soul, and mind, glorifying Your name forever. In Jesus' name, Amen.

A GREATER FAITH

Be on your guard;
stand firm in the faith;
be men of courage;
be strong.

1 Corinthians 16:13

James 1:6-7
Hebrews 11:6
Romans 4:20-21
2 Timothy 1:6-7

Father, shower my wife with an extra dose of faith today. Reveal Yourself to her in mighty and undeniable ways. I pray You will be so apparent to her that her faith cannot rest on man's wisdom, but only in Your great power (1 Corinthians 2:5). May she turn to You in all she does, trusting that You will reward her faithfulness to her. Help her be one of those who earnestly seek You above all else. May her faith continue to grow to new heights as she becomes fully persuaded that You have the power to do exactly what You have said You will (Romans 4:21).

Lord, when my wife asks anything in Your name, help her not doubt You (James 1:6-7). Where she may be wavering, help her unbelief. Strengthen her trust in Your power, Your ways, Your ability, and Your promises. Where she feels weak, display Your strength. When her faith is timid, anoint her with courage and boldness. Where her faith may have grown complacent, renew it like a wildfire, burning and blazing - yearning for more of You. Help her turn her hope and will toward You, Lord. May she become as one of the radiant ones who continually looks to You in all she does (Psalm 34:5).

Do not let any unbelief or doubt outweigh my wife's hope and trust in You so that at the end of her long faith-filled life, she may stand before You and confidently say, "I have fought the good fight, I have finished the race, I have kept the faith" (2 Timothy 4:7). May she be greatly praised at Your Holy City's gates for her steadfastness in You, oh Lord. In Jesus' precious name, Amen.

A BETTER ATTITUDE

Rid yourselves
of all offenses
you have committed
and get a new heart
and a new spirit.

Ezekiel 18:31

Philippians 2:3-8
Romans 12:3
Ezekiel 36:27-28
Titus 3:1-2

Dear heavenly Father, thank You for giving my wife a sound mind (2 Timothy 1:7). I pray You would guard her heart and mind, so that her thoughts and words may be found pleasing in Your sight.

Father, enable my wife to steer her attitude correctly. Remind her often to humble herself before You as Jesus did, taking on the nature of a servant, willing to serve those around her in sacrificial love (Philippians 2:5-8). Lord, give my wife a desire to obey Your Word. Help her be ready to do whatever is good, to avoid slander, to be peaceable and considerate in all that she does, showing true humility toward all people (Titus 3:1-2).

Jesus, it is in Your name that I take a stand against any attitudes of pride or self-righteousness that might be taking root in my wife even now. Pluck out the old mindsets and in their stead, plant new and holy ones, Father. Give her wisdom and grace to honor others before herself, always devoted to those around her in brotherly love (Romans 12:10). Father, continue to work a right spirit within my wife. Renew and refresh her daily, so she may walk as one ready to follow Your will and Your ways all the days of her life. In Jesus' name, Amen.

HER LOVE FOR OTHERS

Love must be sincere.
Hate what is evil;
cling to what is good.
Be devoted to one
another in brotherly love.

Romans 12:9-0

Ephesians 5:1-2
1 Corinthians 13:1-8

Father, I praise You for sending Your Son and giving us the perfect example of love: to love others the way they need to be loved and not how they deserve to be loved. I pray You will put such a love in my wife's heart, a love that's unselfish and doesn't expect compensation.

Father, I pray my wife will do nothing out of selfish ambition or vain conceit, but will, in humility, consider others better than herself. Teach her not to seek her own ways, nor have ulterior motives when she serves others, but to be genuinely concerned about their well-being. Teach her that love is patient and kind, not envious, boastful, proud, rude, or easily angered (1 Corinthians 13:4-8). Help her lay down her will and plans when it is edifying to others to do so. May she see that in humbling herself, she is not giving up or being shamed, but rather through her deference to other people, she is doing a kingdom work that will gain her an eternal reward.

Father, soften my wife's heart toward me and our children. Give her wisdom and understanding, persevering in living out a patient, forgiving love. Help my wife feel Your nearness as she serves in love. Let her experience Your power, overwhelm her and fill her with Yourself so she may spill over with a pure and righteous love.

Father, remind my wife daily that neither life nor death, neither angels nor demons, neither the present nor the future, neither height nor depth, nor anything else in all creation, will be able to separate her from Your great love (Romans 8:38-39). May this knowledge strengthen her and give her an ever increasing desire to walk in obedience to Your command to love as You do. In Jesus' precious name, Amen.

10

FINDING JOY IN TRIALS

I will rejoice in the Lord, I will be joyful in God my Savior. The Sovereign Lord is my strength;... He enables me to go the heights.

Habakkuk 3:18-19

Psalm 13:5-6
Psalm 16:11
Psalm 94:19
Jeremiah 31:13

Dear Heavenly Father, thank You for promising Your strength to us. We find a great and settling joy in being able to rely on You when trials blaze. I pray that Your consolation during the harder times of life will be a source of joy for me and my wife. Do not let us be distraught and burdened beyond what we can bear. Let us rest in knowing You bring nothing that will harm or destroy Your faithful ones.

Father, I pray specifically for my wife, that You would teach her to see trials for what they are: the testing of her faith. Help her endure Your refining work with her eyes and heart focused on Your goodness. Through the trials prove to my wife that You are her strength, her source of joy, and that You enable her to go the heights (Habakkuk 3:18-19). Strengthen her so that she may walk the way You would have her go and succeed in Your plans for her. When she has remained steadfast in You, make her joy greater than her heartache. May she truly rejoice in the growth and maturity she experiences in You.

Lord, help my wife ever trust in You no matter what storm or season she faces. When life is easy for a time, may she see it as a gift from You. Do not let her take it for granted, but continue to prepare her heart and mind in Your Word. When she is crossing turbulent waters, teach her Your unfailing love so she will not be shaken. Lord, grant her eternal blessings and make her glad with the joy Your presence (Psalm 21:6-7). In Jesus' name, Amen.

11

CLAIMING PEACE

You will keep
in perfect peace
him whose mind
is steadfast,
because he
trusts in You.

Isaiah 26:3

Numbers 6:24-26
Psalm 33:20-22
Philippians 4:6-7

Dear Heavenly Father, in this world we are promised trouble, yet in You, we are promised peace. We take heart in the knowledge that You have overcome the world (John 16:33), and that in You we may have peace at all times and in every way (2 Thessalonians 3:16).

Father, when darts of the evil one are being fired from all directions, keep my wife's mind steadfast on You desiring Your peace and Your presence. Help her to not be anxious about anything, but in everything, make her requests known to You through prayer and petition (Philippians 4:6-7). Impart peace beyond measure upon her, reassuring her that You are not slack in keeping Your promises. May Your blessed assurance keep her from succumbing to the temptations of despair, hopelessness, depression, or distrust in You.

Father, move my wife's heart to promote peace in all she does. Help her overcome the temptations to be quick to argue or seek revenge. It is to an individual's honor to avoid strife, but every fool is quick to quarrel (Proverbs 20:3). Lord, You have not made my wife to live foolishly, but to be a woman of courageous faith. Help her be kind, patient, and loving, making every effort to do what leads to peace and mutual edification of those around her (Romans 14:19).

May my wife's heart overflow with Your peace, Father, and spill out of her life for all to see. May all she does be done to promote Your will and agenda. I stand on behalf of my wife and ask that You pour Your peace into her heart. Help her rest in the reality that she is dearly loved by You through all of life's ups and downs. In Jesus' name, Amen.

GROWING IN PATIENCE

A man's wisdom
gives him patience;
it is to his glory
to overlook an offense.

Proverbs 19:11

Colossians 1:9-12
Colossians 3:12-13
1 Thessalonians 5:14
James 1:2-4

Father, thank You for being a patient God. Thank You that Your mercies are never ending. I pray You will give my wife and I hearts that are patient and understanding, willing to go the distance of bearing with each other. Your Word tells us our wisdom gives us great patience and that it is to our glory to overlook an offense (Proverbs 19:11). Lord, may this gracious attitude be a mutual gift my wife and I extend to each other. Anoint us with wisdom and help us choose patience in all circumstances.

Father, I lift my wife to You and ask that You work in her to let go of any impatience, grudges, anger, jealous tendencies or harsh words. In their place, teach her to be completely humble and gentle, bearing with others in love (Ephesians 4:2). When people are difficult or plans don't turn out as expected, give her an accepting attitude. Help her see that Your way is never wrong and that the testing of her faith will invariably include the testing of her patience. May she clothe herself with kindness and compassion (Colossians 3:12-13), ever persevering in doing what is good.

Lord, fill my wife with the knowledge of Your will through all spiritual wisdom and understanding. I stand praying that by Your power she will live a life worthy of You. May she please You in every way: bearing fruit in every good work, growing in the knowledge of God, and being strengthened according to Your glorious might so that she may have great endurance to run the race marked out before her (Colossians 1:9-11). In Jesus' precious name, Amen.

13

PRACTICING KINDNESS

A kind man benefits himself,
but a cruel man brings
trouble on himself.

Proverbs 11:17

Daniel 4:27
Romans 11:22
Proverbs 14:31
2 Peter 1:5-8

Father, thank You for Your kindness. Your mercies are never ending, reaching even to the ungrateful and wicked. Teach my wife to be kind to others, to love her enemies and do good to them (Luke 6:35). May she never pay back wrong for wrong, but always be kind to all people (1 Thessalonians 5:15).

Father, I pray You would move my wife's heart to rid herself of any bitterness, rage, anger, brawling, slander or any other form of malice. In their stead, grow her to be kind and compassionate toward others, forgiving others as You have forgiven her (Ephesians 4:31-32). May she not have ulterior motives for extending kindness, but may true compassion permeate all her words and actions.

Thank you, Lord, that I am often the recipient of my wife's kindness. Help me show the same to her, living with her in ways that will cause her to feel cherished, treasured, and safe with me. Grow me more gentle in my words and dealings with my wife.

Lord, I pray that You would make my wife prosperous in all she does. May the work of her hands demonstrate the beauty of her heart and may she be greatly rewarded for her upright and pure life. May my wife's life as a workman approved by God, claim for her long term peace of mind and good reputation. In Jesus' name, Amen.

14

BECOMING GOOD

Test everything.
Hold on to the good.
Avoid every kind of evil.

1 Thessalonians 5:21-22

1 Peter 2:12
Proverbs 22:1
Jeremiah 6:16

Dear Jesus, thank You for the good You have shown my wife and me throughout our marriage. Thank you for the times You kept us from making bad choices; the times You've intervened to save our lives, souls, and reputations. Help us see that the favor that You have shown us is not of our own doing, but a provision from You.

Father, I pray you would grow my wife and I in our attempts to show goodness toward each other. Help my wife not seek her own good or be selfish in her motives. Likewise, remind me continually to seek the greater good of my wife and other people (1 Corinthians 10:24).

Help my wife work toward mutual edification in all situations, so that even pagans can see Your work of goodness through her (1 Peter 2:12). Father, I pray You would impress upon my wife to continue leading a disciplined life and to be clear minded and self-controlled. May she not grow weary in doing what is right, for at the proper time You promise a harvest if she doesn't give up (Galatians 6:9-10). Do not let her grow slack, weak-willed, or complacent. Instead, surround her with Your strength and help her walk in ways that are pleasing to You.

Father, help my wife to seek You first and by the constant use of your Word, train herself in godliness. Lord, when she is at the crossroads of good and evil, pour out Your wisdom and discernment upon her so she may know the way that is good. Then, may Your peace surround her, encouraging her to go the way of uprightness. Lead her, guide her, and direct her in the way that is good. In Jesus' name, Amen.

15

HER FAITHFULNESS

Love the Lord,
all His faithful people!
The Lord preserves
those who are true to Him,
but the proud
He pays back in full.

Psalm 31:23

Psalm 18:25-36
Ephesians 6:10-18
1 Corinthians 4:2

Jesus, thank You for Your faithfulness, even to the cross. You have proven to be our Rock. All Your ways are perfect and just. You, O Lord, are a compassionate and gracious God, slow to anger, abounding in love and faithfulness (Psalm 86:15).

I pray You would give my wife an abundant desire to grow in Your likeness. Teach her to be a woman of courageous faith, standing for what is good and right in Your eyes. I pray she will be on her guard against anything that does not bring life and godliness. Make righteousness to be her belt and faithfulness the sash around her waist (Isaiah 11:5). Help her bear up under the armor You provide by girding herself in truth, so she may be able to discern good from evil. Help her be wise to the ways of the world and the lord of it, the enemy.

Father, give my wife the courage to apply Your standard to all of life's circumstances so that she may be known as a woman after Your own heart. When the road is dark before her, help her put on the shoes of peace so that she may not be frightened. May she stand strong in faith, claiming her status in You. Lord, make my wife a woman pure in thought and deed, always being guided by Your Word so that she may live holy and blameless before You.

Father, now I lay open our marriage before You. Help us stand strong using the Sword of the Spirit, Your Word, as our guide and protection against temptation. May we not yield to anything that could blemish our lives or compromise our marriage covenant. Help us renounce anything that does not bring honor and glory to You. Grow our love for You to be greater than our love for each other, for in that way we may be strengthened to remain faithful to each other. In Jesus' name, Amen.

PRACTICING SELF-CONTROL

So then,
let us not be like others,
who are asleep,
but let us be alert and
self-controlled.

1 Thessalonians 5:6

Proverbs 16:32
1 Peter 1:13
Proverbs 29:11
Titus 2:12

Father God, I come before You, thankful for this woman You have put in my life; this beautiful creation You have called me to love, honor and help. I thank You that You have made her a woman able to discern right from wrong. Help her see where practicing more self-control would benefit her life and our union. Keep renewing her mind, enlightening her, and showing her Your will and Your way.

Father, as the heart of our marriage and family, I pray my wife would be a workman worthy of what You have called her to do. Remove any tendencies to be demanding or quick tempered. May she not be given to drunkenness, violence, gossip, slander, or lies. Restore in her hospitality; make her good, self-controlled, upright, holy, and disciplined, ever holding firm to Your trustworthy way (Titus 1:7-9). Give her insight so she may know where she may need to correct any inward feelings of bitterness, anger, or pride.

Father, I pray my wife will not be as some who sleep, spiritually speaking, but that she may remain alert and self-controlled, putting on faith and love as a breastplate, and the hope of salvation as a helmet (1 Thessalonians 5:6-8). I pray that You would strengthen and uphold my wife making her able to resist the darts of temptation fired at her.

Jesus, You are the perfect example of a life lived clear minded and self-controlled. Teach my wife to be the same: temperate, worthy of respect, faithful, loving and patient, doing what is good, showing integrity in all she does by her seriousness and soundness of speech. May those who oppose her be ashamed because they can find nothing bad to say about her. Through Your great grace, teach her to reject ungodliness and worldly passions, and to clothe herself with self-control, living an upright and godly life. In Jesus' name, Amen.

17

SEEKING WISDOM

The fear of the Lord
is the beginning of wisdom;
all who have His precepts
have good understanding.

Psalm 111:10

Proverbs 11:2
James 1:5
1 Kings 3:9
Proverbs 8:10-11

Father, You have promised to give wisdom where it is asked (James 1:5). I ask that You would give my wife a heart that can discern. Help her understand Your Word. Give her Your precepts and impart wisdom to her so she may know what is Your good and perfect will.

Father, I pray you will teach my wife to not be wise in her own eyes, doing whatever she wants, but to always seek You first, wanting to please You above man. Help her understand that looking to You first will bring health and nourishment to her body (Proverbs 3:7-8).

Father, we know wisdom is found in those who take advice and accept instruction (Proverbs 13:10, 19:20). Make my wife one who is capable of accepting advice from others. Where You would like to purge any pride or self inspired agendas, convict her gently to renew her mind and heart. Lord, do not let her be so set in her ways that she will scoff in the face of others who mean well. Rather, let her thoughtfully and patiently consider their words. Anoint her with wisdom and reveal truth, even when it's not what she wants to hear.

Father, deepen my wife's desire to grow in Your Word. It has been said, the Holy Scriptures are able to make you wise (2 Timothy 3:15). I ask again that You would impart great wisdom to my wife, so that she may lay a foundation of faith for generations to come. Help her act justly, love mercy, and walk humbly before You, our unchangeable, infallible, sovereign Lord (Micah 6:8). In Jesus' name, Amen.

18

DEVELOPING INTEGRITY

The man of integrity walks securely, but he who takes crooked paths will be found out.

Proverbs 10:9

Isaiah 32:8
Proverbs 27:12
Psalm 25:21
Psalm 26:11-12

Dear Jesus, thank You for the perfect example of a life of integrity. You did everything with a sincere love for mankind and humble obedience to Your Father. I pray You will reveal Your goodness to my wife and give her the desire to follow in Your example.

Lord, give my wife a heart that is sincere, hating what is evil, clinging to what is good (Romans 12:9). Many are the plans of a person's heart, but I pray, Lord, that You would direct the plans of my wife's heart into noble ones. If the plans of her heart do not fit into Your will or do not line up with Your Word, do not let them come about. Keep her from doing anything that will lead to regret, guilt, or a tarnished reputation. May integrity and uprightness protect her (Psalm 25:21). May she always go the way of integrity, being irreproachable, with sound speech that cannot be condemned (Titus 2:7-8).

Father, I pray You would impart wisdom and prudence upon my dear wife so she may always know and decide what is right. Should she tempted to do something not glorifying to You, help her stand strong in her faith and walk in the way that is right. May she be among those who have clean hands and a pure heart, who will one day be rewarded by dwelling in Your presence (Psalm 24:3-4). May she ever seek to lead a blameless life before You. In Jesus' name, Amen.

KEEPING HONEST

The Lord detests lying lips,
but He delights in men
who are truthful.

Proverbs 12:22

Psalm 24:3-4
Proverbs 19:9
1 Peter 3:10-12

Father, we know You do not lie and that You hate all things deceitful. Anyone who practices deceit will not dwell in Your house; anyone who speaks falsely will not stand before You (Psalm 101:7). Untruths are one of the seven abominations and those who partake in it will not go unpunished (Proverbs 6:16). I pray You will remove from my wife any lying or deceptive tendencies. Make her a woman who hates dishonesty in life and speech as much as You do.

Father, I pray You would give my wife the desire to always speak truthfully and sincerely. May she refuse to let deceit spill from her lips, always speaking truth in love. Help my wife walk in the goal of purity and uprightness, keeping to truth even when it hurts (Psalm 15:4). May she be known as one whose "Yes" is "Yes" and her "No" is "No" (Matthew 5:37).

I pray my wife would be a woman who is honest in all her dealings, whether in business, ministry, or home. You, oh Lord, detest differing weights and dishonest scales (Proverbs 20:23), so place my wife in right standing with God and man, so that no one may find fault in her dealings.

Father, I pray that You would keep the intentions of my wife's heart pleasing in Your sight (Psalm 19:14). May she always keep growing in You, seeking to live a life that is transparent and pure. In Jesus' name, Amen.

20

HUMILITY: A WAY OF LIFE

Do not think of yourself more highly than you ought, but rather think of yourself with sober judgment.

Romans 12:3

Proverbs 15:31-33
Proverbs 16:5,
Isaiah 66:2
Matthew 23:12
James 4:10

Father, we know You hate the proud and love the humble. You have instructed us to not think of ourselves more highly than we ought to, but to think of ourselves with sober judgment (Romans 12:3). Grow my wife into a woman who doesn't think herself better than those around her. Give her a heart that is willing to honor others above herself. May she serve others without ulterior motives, selfish ambitions, or vain conceit. Instead, grow her to be humble and gracious, willing to contribute to the good of others (Philippians 2:3-4).

Father, teach my wife to be careful of the words she speaks and thinks of herself. You do not find boasting good or of any worth (1 Corinthians 5:6). Your Word tells us that whoever exalts themselves will be humbled, and whoever humbles themselves will be exalted (Matthew 23:12). Before a downfall comes pride (Proverbs 18:12). Do not let my wife be a woman brought to destruction, shame, or disgrace due to boastful words, selfish actions, or a proud heart. Let others praise her and not herself (Proverbs 27:2).

Lord, I pray also that my wife would see herself as You do and not think of herself in harmful or demeaning ways. Help her recognize that You have designed her perfectly for the call You have on her life, and will fully equip her in those things. Lord, when self destructive thoughts threaten to take over, help her counter them with truth. Help her understand it is good and right to walk in the beauty you have designed in her. May she come to see humility as power under control, and walk confidently in the way You have made her.

Father, You promise to supply the meek with wealth, honor, life, and wisdom (Proverbs 22:4; 11:2). Develop in my wife a heart that is not proud and eyes that are not haughty (Psalm 131:1). Teach her that meekness is obedience to You, always ready to do whatever is good, to slander no one and to be peaceable and considerate, showing true humility toward all people (Titus 3:1-2). Teach her not fret herself with things that seem great and wonderful on this earth, but instead to quiet her soul before You and put her hope in You both now and forevermore (Psalm 131:1-3) In Jesus' name, Amen.

Colossians 3:19

Husbands,
love your wives
and do not be
harsh with them.

COURAGE FOR THE WAY

Be strong and courageous,
and do the work.
Do not be afraid
or discouraged,
for the Lord your God,
my God, is with you.
He will not fail or forsake you.

1 Chronicles 28:20

Psalm 27:14
Deuteronomy 31:6
Isaiah 12:2

Father, thank You that You make us courageous beyond our abilities. You promise to always be with us to guide us, direct us, comfort us and strengthen us. I pray that You will give my wife an extra measure of this assurance today. Help her be on her guard and stand firm in the faith (1 Corinthians 16:13). Father, You have not given my wife a spirit of timidity, but a spirit of power, of love, and of self-discipline. Do not let her be ashamed to testify about You by choosing to stand against evil (2 Timothy 1:7-8).

Father, when my wife deals with difficult people or situations, help her not be intimidated into silence or fear. Instead, make her strong and courageous, not fearing or being in dread of others. Remind her often that it is You with her and that You will never leave her or forsake her (Deuteronomy 31:6). Help her stand and conduct herself in a manner worthy of the gospel, knowing that You will preserve her life no matter what is placed in her path.

Lord, give my wife courage to always do what is right in Your eyes. Help her trust You with all her heart and not lean on her own understanding (Proverbs 3:5). Do not let her grow discouraged. Instead, make her willing to walk in ways that please You even when it's hard. Remind her that You notice and that You reward Your faithful servant. Make my wife a pillar of courage, standing strong on Your foundation calmly weathering the storms around her. In Jesus' name, Amen.

22

REPENTANCE AND FORGIVING OTHERS

When forgiveness is needed, Lord, help me be the first to the cross.

Amen.

Isaiah 43:25
Proverbs 19:11
Proverbs 28:13
Matthew 6:14-15

Father, thank You for Your great mercy. You have shown it to all generations. You are a forgiving God; gracious and compassionate, slow to anger, abounding in love (Nehemiah 9:17). You have promised that when Your people turn from their sins and seek Your face, You will hear them and will be faithful to forgive and heal them (1 John 1:9).

Father, I pray You will give my wife a heart that willingly turns to You. Give her the courage to admit any wrong she may have done. Cultivate in her an ongoing, ever-strengthening desire to do what is good and pleasing in Your eyes. When You convict my wife, Father, also move her to humble repentance, seeing her sin as You do and fully renouncing its hold on her life.

Father, in her repentance give her Your peace so she may know that she is fully forgiven and may walk unashamedly before You. Assure her that You have removed her sin as far as the east is from the west and that You are the one Who blots out her transgressions and will remember them no more (Isaiah 43:25).

Father, as You have forgiven my wife of any confessed sin, also give her a heart to forgive others. Teach her that she must forgive in order to be forgiven and that You forgive with the same measure she forgives (Matthew 6:14-15). Soften my wife's heart toward anyone who treats her poorly, bearing with everyone in love. Be her Rock when it's hard to see past the pain, the unfairness, or the human tendency to seek revenge.

I pray also, Father, that You would help my wife and me make forgiveness a lifestyle. Where there have been disappointments, blame, bitterness, hardness of heart, grudges or contention, help us heal through the power of forgiveness. Renew in us a willingness to be patient and understanding toward one another. Help us forgive quickly, overlooking offenses and not using them against each other. Heal us Father, and guard us in Your love. In Jesus' name, Amen.

23

TRUSTING GOD FOR HIS PROMISES

But blessed is the man
who trusts in the Lord,
whose confidence is in Him.

Jeremiah 17:7

Psalm 119:137-138
Psalm 62:5-8
Isaiah 25:9
Psalm 56:3-4,

Father, we know Your ways are good and perfect. Your Word is flawless and You promise to be a shield to those who trust in You (2 Samuel 22:31). Today I pray my wife would be dealt an extra measure of belief. Show her throughout the day that she can trust You with whatever comes. Where there is even a small measure of distrust, doubt, or trepidation, remind her that You have proven Yourself faithful since the beginning of time and You promise to remain trustworthy into all eternity.

Father, when my wife makes plans that go wrong or don't hold out, do not let her become discouraged. Remind her that this is only for a season, and that when she stands firmly on Your solid foundation You will greatly reward her. Many are the woes of the wicked, but Your unfailing love surrounds those who trust in You (Psalm 32:10). Teach my wife to know that Your thoughts and Your ways are above all others, and that You cannot allow what is not fitting to Your great plan (Isaiah 55:8-9). Let my wife find peace and rest in the promise that Your great and wonderful plans will prevail.

Father, I pray You will also make my wife a woman who can be trusted. Keep growing her in ways that are honorable, so that she may be proven by her good works as a woman who is genuine and honest. I praise You, Lord, that You have given her a sound mind and teachable heart. Speak to her daily through Your Word and Spirit. With Your perfect guidance, may my wife continue becoming a woman walking in wisdom, her confidence secured in You (Proverbs 28:26, Jeremiah 17:7). In Jesus' name, Amen.

24

HEARING THE LORD

Lord,
help me hear Your voice
guiding me in paths
that are pleasing to You.

Amen.

James 1:22
Proverbs 18:15
Matthew 7:26
Mark 4:20

Father, I praise You for the wisdom that You willingly pour out to those who ask (James 1:5). Today I pray my wife will not only ask for and seek wisdom, but that she may hear from You clearly and correctly, also. May her ears be opened, always inclined to hear from You through Your Word and Spirit.

Jesus, You have said, "But everyone who hears these words of mine and does not put them into practice is like a foolish man who built his house on sand" (Matthew 7:26). May my wife be far from being one of those who hear Your Word yet never do as it directs. You have not given her a heart that cannot be molded and taught, nor ears that cannot hear Your Word. Remove all foolishness and self-centered tendencies, and replace them with attitudes of love and growth. Open her spiritual ears so that she may know Your voice ever more intimately. Whisper to her things of beauty and encouragement, preparing her for the things you are orchestrating in her life.

Father, also open my wife's ears to good instruction, knowledge, and sound teaching. Open her ears to words of rebuke, correction and chastisement as well. While receiving such words is never easy, it is necessary for growth. Give my wife discernment as she gives the words of correction thoughtful consideration. Make all discipline that is from You be like an ornament of fine gold to her listening ears (Proverbs 25:12). Help her recognize advice given in love and take action on anything that needs improvement.

Father, I pray all sound guidance and insight will fall on the good soil of my wife's heart. Help her hear Your words, accept Your words, and produce an abundant harvest through her obedience to You (Mark 4:20). In Jesus' precious name, Amen.

25

OBEDIENCE WHEN CALLED

Jesus replied,
"If anyone loves me,
he will obey my teaching."

John 14:23

Psalm 119:88
Deuteronomy 13:3-4
Deuteronomy 30:9-10

Sweet Jesus, You are a gentle presence. You are kind. You are patient. You are loving. You are also sovereign and cannot tolerate the sin of disobedience. Prove Yourself trustworthy to my wife so she may learn to love and obey Your commands without hesitation.

Lord, we know You test us to see whether we love You with all our heart and soul (Deuteronomy 13:3-4). When You test my wife do so gently so she will not become overwhelmed. When walking through times of testing grant her the peace that passes all understanding, reminding her that she is not alone in this journey.

Father, do not let my wife grow angry at You or weary of Your will and Your ways. I pray she will obey the commands You have written to us and that she will turn to You with all her heart and all her soul. When doubt knocks and she feels like giving up, pour into her enough faith and courage to stand strong and say, "I will obey my God's teaching." Then, in due time, bless her abundantly for her devotion to You.

Father, I pray also that my wife's example of humble obedience will direct the course of our children's lives and many generations after them. Today, freshen her faith and her resolve to serve You and bring her life in compliance with Your will. In Jesus' precious name, Amen.

26

HER SUBMISSIVE LEADERSHIP

Lord,
help me lead in ways
that make it a joy
for my wife to
live her life with me.

Amen.

Deuteronomy 6:5-8
1 Peter 3:7
Proverbs 17:27
Mark 10:42-45

Father, I praise You for the work You are doing in my wife's life. Teach her to love Your Word more and more so that she will be able to lead her life in ways that will draw her others to You.

Where biblical submission was not modeled to my wife, provide godly role models for her to fashion her life after. Teach her through Your Word that true submission is not being a doormat, but rather a powerful and leadership driven position.

Father, where I have held a superior and harmful stance on the idea of what submission is, please forgive me. Help me not "lord it over" my wife, making her feel less than, inferior, or pathetic. Give me the humility and courage to reconcile with my wife and seek her forgiveness as well. Remove any pride I have in a self proclaimed status as husband and protector, so I might lead my wife to a more complete understanding of her place in Your design.

Father, do not let my wife be intimidated by the call You have given her as submissive leader of her home. Rather, give her the courage, ability, and ease to walk out this calling in all wisdom and confidence. Give her wisdom where she needs to speak up and peace where she feels led to remain silent. Help me as her husband to truly listen to her words and desires, not dismissing them as a nuisance.

Lord, I pray that You would give my wife a refreshed desire and joy to live her life with me in our marriage covenant. Help us submit to one another in love, honoring one another above ourselves, giving each other the understanding we want given to ourselves.

Father, I pray my wife would stand strong in the power of Your might. Do not let her wane in her faith but always keeping her prepared to do what You require. May Your ways and what is edifying to growth be what her life is marked by. May she lead with wisdom, integrity and servant-hood in her home, workplace, friendships, and marriage. In Jesus' precious name, Amen.

27

PURPOSEFUL MOTHERHOOD

Lord, make motherhood a joy for my wife.

Amen.

Ephesians 6:4
Colossians 3:21
Proverbs 22:6
Isaiah 40:11

Father in heaven, thank You for a beautiful picture of what a parent looks like; not harsh yet commanding respect, not demanding yet expecting obedience, not irrational in ways that exasperate Your children but always loving, always kind, and ever gracious. Give my wife Your heart toward her children. Make her a woman who communicates unconditional love to them so they may always know they are loved.

Help her be patient with her children, Father. Show her the grace You have covered her with so that she may, in turn, extend grace to her children. When she feels impatient, help her rise above the immediate circumstances, enabling her to speak and respond in ways she won't regret. Help her speak with calmness and authority, never letting her children doubt her love for them.

Father, show my wife where she can cultivate a deeper relationship with each child. I pray she will not be cold, harsh, uninterested, undependable, or neglectful. May she never provoke her children to wrath, but bring them up in the training and admonition of You, Lord (Ephesians 6:4). Help her be present physically and emotionally, not being ruled by what she might deem of greater importance right at that moment.

Where she feels inadequate to teach her children Your ways, Lord, give her courage and the ability to speak what they need to hear. Help her communicate Your ways to them. May the knowledge that their mother loves the Almighty have a profound impact on their lives.

Father, we know You discipline those You love (Proverbs 3:12). You do it with great love, mercy, and the desire to grow us up in You. When disciplining her own children, help my wife do so calmly, justly, and lovingly, never in anger, irritation or self-righteousness. Help her be a fair judge, not dealing with them in haste. Where reconciliation with a child would benefit their relationship, help my wife be a humble example in seeking forgiveness.

Father, I pray you will lead my wife with each step in this journey called motherhood. Guide her and direct her paths in ways that will make this role a pleasure for her. May she find great fulfillment in raising her children for You, and when she is old and gray may she rest, knowing she obediently left a rich spiritual inheritance for her children. In Jesus' precious name, Amen.

10 Psalms for Godly Character

LOVE
Psalm 86:1-17

JOY
Psalm 16:1-11

PEACE
Psalm 23:1-6

PATIENCE
Psalm 62:1-12

KINDNESS
Psalm 116:1-19

GOODNESS
Psalm 18:1-36

FAITHFULNESS
Psalm 143:1-12

SELF-CONTROL
Psalm 37:1-11

WISDOM
Psalm 1:1-6

HUMILITY
Psalm 51:1-19

28

HER WORK AND GIFTS

Commit to the Lord
whatever you do,
and your plans
will succeed.

Proverbs 16:3

Colossians 3:23
Ecclesiastes 5:18-19
1 Timothy 5:8
1 Thessalonians 4:11-12

Father, bless my wife's work. Thank you for giving her the abilities to do the work You have called her to. Help her find a proper balance between working too much and being too lazy to take on her responsibilities.

Father, I pray she may work with her own hands so that she will not grow completely dependent on anybody (1 Thessalonians 4:11-12). I pray she will make it her ambition to lead a quiet and simple life so that her daily work may win the respect of outsiders. Teach her to bring You into every aspect of her day's work and activities. Where there is anything not glorifying to You, convict her, then supply her with the courage to make any necessary changes. Teach her to commit whatever she does to You, so her plans may succeed (Proverbs 16:3).

Lord, You have also given my wife specific gifts. I pray that she will flourish in her gifts, finding great fulfillment in the things she loves and dreams of. Help her find balance between her callings and where you have placed her right now. Do not let her become frustrated or overloaded. Help her find focus and clarity on what is truly from You and in Your perfect timing. Lord, help me be supportive of her activities and pursuits. Make me the encouraging, steady hand she can lean on when she is weary or overwhelmed.

Father, I pray for the individuals You bring into my wife's life through her daily work or callings. May they be people of integrity who encourage and strengthen her walk with You. Guide my wife away from anyone or anything that could harm her mentally or physically. Steer my wife away from bad business deals, jobs, or influences that could rob her peace or reputation.

Father, help me to not come in the way of Your will for my wife's work and callings. I confess the times I haven't been supportive or appreciative of the way she is gifted. Help me accept her journey in life, knowing You are the one weaving her life, all the while guiding and protecting her. I firmly hold on to the promise that You are faithful to Your faithful ones.

Continue to grow her into Your faithful one and giving me the wisdom to encourage and affirm her.

Father, lead us, guide us, and direct us. Then surround us, encourage us, and enable us to do our life's work humbly, willingly, and thoroughly. Each for You first while fitting into each other's lives perfectly. May we both be strong and courageous, willing to do the work you call us to and to lay down our lives for the betterment of the other. In Jesus' name, Amen.

Courage Scripture Readings

Isaiah 33:2-6

Psalm 56:1-13

Psalm 18:1-6

Psalm 18:16-24

Psalm 18:25-36

Psalm 62:1-8

Hebrews 2:14- 3:6

Romans 8:28-39

Deuteronomy 20:1-4

Psalm 138:1-8

29

CONFIDENCE IN HER CALLINGS

The fruit of righteousness will be peace; the effect of righteousness will be quietness and confidence forever.

Isaiah 32:17

Psalm 29:11
Psalm 55:22
Proverbs 3:25-26
Hebrew 10:35-36

Dear Jesus, thank you for this woman you have given me. I pray she would come to see herself as You see her – beautiful, complete, whole, and dearly loved. Lord, give her the confidence she needs to go throughout her day. Help her walk boldly in Your love. May she feel Your strength surrounding her even now, enabling her to walk in confidence and assurance.

Lord, give my wife a quieted heart. May she be convinced of Your love, how deep and wide, strong and endless it is for her (Romans 8:37-38). Lord, when you call her to do something, double her portion of perseverance. Give her the peace that only comes when we know that we are in Your will (Isaiah 32:17)

Lord, where there is even a shadow of a doubt in my wife, remove it from her quickly. Do not let her fear. Be her confidence and do not let her become ensnared by the enemy's plans to swarm her with anxiety. I stand in the gap, Lord, asking that You hold back the flood of insecurities that threaten my wife's heart, mind, and soul. Make her strong in You, willing to do the work You have called her to without hesitation. Enable her to go the heights You have ordained for her.

Lord, help my wife see her value, worth, and influence. You have made her in Your image, Lord, and in You she is powerful and sure-footed. Help her hold on to the hope You have called her to, so that she may be richly rewarded when she has persevered in Your will (Hebrews 10:35).

Father, I pray everything my wife does will be pleasing in Your sight, that her efforts may be multiplied, and every step she takes may be right and blessed. In Jesus name, Amen.

30

PROTECTION FOR THE DAY

"Because he loves me,"
says the Lord,
"I will rescue him,
I will protect him,
for he acknowledges
my name."

Psalm 91:14

Psalm 34:22
Psalm 91:9-11
Psalm 18:1-3
Psalm 32:6-7
Psalm 121:7-8

Father, I thank You for the promises of safety You give throughout the Bible. You give us refuge. You are our strength and redeemer. Thank You that You will never leave us nor forsake us and that you will be gracious to us all the days of our lives.

Father, protect my wife in all the ways she walks; watch over her coming and going (Psalm 121:8), guiding her away from any harmful situations. Protect her from traveling accidents, work accidents, sicknesses, and harmful diseases of the body or mind. Protect her from violence and the people who do it. Lord, I know that Your arm is not too short that You cannot save (Isaiah 59:1). Preserve the life of my wife so that we might grow old together and watch our children's children grow. I entrust her to You, fully convinced that You are able to protect her today and every day of her life (2 Timothy 1:12).

Father, when my wife's heart is burdened and the world seems dark all around her, remind her that You are her shield, deliverer, and rock. Remind her that You are the firm foundation, cornerstone, and stronghold (2 Samuel 22:1-4). Protect her from any attacks the enemy plans to make on her mind and body. I stand on behalf of my wife and by faith in Jesus Christ divert the fiery darts that get sent her way. The enemy has no right to her. She is in the lineage of the Living God who promises to protect and preserve His children.

Father, I stand in the gap on behalf of our marriage (Ezekiel 22:30-31), asking that You shower the blood of Jesus over us and our marriage that we may be protected spiritually, physically, emotionally, and sexually by Your great power and love. In Jesus' precious name, Amen.

31

A WORTHY EXAMPLE

Be shepherds of God's flock
that is under your care,
...not greedy for money,
but eager to serve;
not lording it over
those entrusted to you,
but being examples
to the flock.

1 Peter 5:2-3

Ephesians 5:1-2
1 Timothy 4:12
2 Timothy 2:15-16, 22-24

Dear Jesus, You have set a perfect example for us to follow; one of love, kindness, and humble obedience. Give my wife a desire to fashion her life after Yours, doing nothing out of vain conceit but considering others better than herself (Philippians 2:3). Remind her often that she has younger eyes watching her, looking up to her for guidance. Outside her home, remind her there are worldly eyes watching and needing an example of purity, goodness, and compassion toward mankind.

Father, give my wife strength and courage to do her best to set a good example. Teach her that setting a respectable example includes watching the words she speaks, avoiding godless chatter, gossip, and having nothing to do with foolish and stupid arguments. Teach her that a woman of good character sets an honorable standard when she refuses to quarrel, but instead is kind to everyone (2 Timothy 2:24).

Father, I pray my wife will leave a path worthy of following by the way she conducts herself. Remove any tendencies to be quick-tempered, for we know a person of quick temper does foolish things (Proverbs 14:17). Do not let her be foolish; remove any drunkenness, violence, dishonesty or any evil tendencies of the heart. In their place, teach her to be hospitable, and love what is good, to be self-controlled, upright, holy and disciplined. Help her live a blameless life, setting an honorable example to all (Titus 1:7-8).

Father, where my wife may have been less than exemplary, give her courage to repent and do better. I fervently pray that where a godly life has not been modeled to her, You would help her rise above and not fall into the traps of generations past. When she is unsure of the best thing to do, move her heart to dig into Your Word, the only good, right and perfect example for her to fashion her life after. May she call upon You and pray to You, seeking You with all her heart until she finds You (Jeremiah 29:12-13). In Jesus' name, Amen.

32

THE PATHS SHE WALKS

Lord,
order my steps,
that I may walk
and lead in
Your power.

Amen.

Psalm 15:1-2
Proverbs 4:26-27
Micah 6:8
Philippians 3:13-15

Father, guide my wife's steps to walk in truth. Give her the courage to turn to right paths that lead to You and are led by You. May she be a woman who learns to acclaim You and who walks in the light of Your presence (Psalm 89:15). I know You count blessed the one "who does not walk in the counsel of the wicked or stand in the way of sinners or sit in the seat of mockers" (Psalm 1:1). Today, convict and guide my wife away from any counsel that is not of You. Let her not take part in the activities of evil-doers, but rather have the courage to walk away from temptations.

Lord, we know those "who walk with the wise grows wise" (Proverbs 13:20). Send my wife along paths that will lead to relationships that help her grow wiser, more humble, and stronger in You. Father, teach my wife to be a woman who will do what You require of her: "to act justly and to love mercy and to walk humbly" before You (Micah 6:8).

Lord, Your command to walk in love is not grievous. Give my wife a heart that is gentle and loving to all she meets today, letting her love for You shine bright and true. May she walk honestly and humbly, having a clear vision of the path You would have her take. Bless her with clarity and courage when You instruct her in the paths she is to take. Father, You move the hearts of kings, so You will also move the heart of my wife to walk rightly, surely, and lovingly.

Encourage her to walk in truth, and to do so quickly. Teach her to seek Your guidance first and foremost, knowing You will never mislead. Help my wife abide in Your tabernacle and dwell on Your holy hill as she walks uprightly and works righteousness and speaks truth in her heart (Psalm 15:1-2).

At the end of her long life, Father, may she look back and praising You, say, "I have kept my feet from every evil path so that I might obey Your Word. I have not departed from Your laws, for You Yourself have taught me" (Psalm 119:101-102). I pray You will continue teaching my wife to understand Your precepts and that she will hate every wrong path.

Strengthen her resolve to seek wisdom from Your Word: the very lamp to our feet and the light for our path (Psalm 119:105). May she always walk worthy of her calling, with all lowliness and gentleness, with long-suffering, and by bearing with all people in love (Ephesians 4:1-2). In Jesus' name, Amen.

Psalm 18:1-2

I love you, O Lord, my **STRENGTH**.

The Lord is my **ROCK**, my **FORTRESS**

and my **DELIVERER**;

my God is my rock,

in whom I take **REFUGE**.

He is my **SHIELD**

and the horn of my **SALVATION**,

my **STRONGHOLD**.

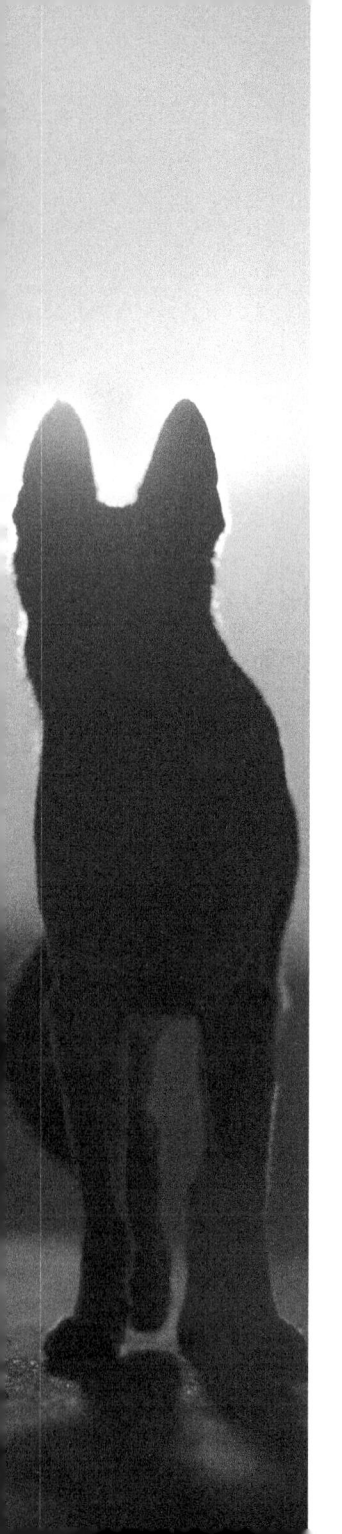

33

THE WORDS SHE SPEAKS

He who guards
his mouth and
his tongue keeps
himself from calamity.

Proverbs 21:23

Proverbs 14:3
Ephesians 5:4
Colossians 3:8
James 1:19-20

Father, words are powerful. They carry life or death, blessing or curses, peace or dissension.

We know that out of the abundance of the heart the mouth speaks (Matthew 12:34). Make my wife's heart pure so that what comes out of her mouth is edifying to You. Do not let unwholesome talk come out of her mouth, but only what is helpful for building others up according to their needs (Ephesians 4:29).

Your Word tells us that there is more hope for a fool than a person who is hasty with their words (Proverbs 29:20). So when my wife feels like spewing anger or frustration, nudge her conscience and halt the words before they are uttered. Give her a gentle and patient spirit so that speaking kindly will become natural to her.

Grow the desire in her to think through her words before she speaks. I command away from her mind all negative thoughts that could result in unwholesome talk to others or about others. I take a stand against all evil spirits that encourage cussing, harsh words, uncaring words, or indifferent words. Give her the courage and strength to rid herself of anger, rage, malice, slander, filthy language, and to avoid godless chatter, knowing all those things will only lead to more ungodliness.

Instead of obscenity, foolish talk or coarse joking, convict my wife to speak with thanksgiving (Ephesians 5:4). Let her conversation always be full of grace, seasoned with salt, so she will always know how to answer everyone according to Your Word (Colossians 4:6). May the words of her mouth and the meditation of her heart be ever pleasing to You (Psalm 19:14). In Jesus' name, Amen.

34

COVERING HER CHOICES

All a man's ways
seem right to him,
but the Lord
weighs the heart.

Proverbs 21:2

Proverbs 19:20-21
Joshua 24:15
Deuteronomy 30:9-10, 19-20

Father, once again I praise You that You have given my wife the ability to make wise choices based on Your Word. You have said, "I have set before you life and death, blessings and curses. Now choose life so that you and your children may live, and that you may love the Lord your God, listen to Him and hold fast to Him" (Deuteronomy 30:19-20). Father, move my wife's heart to choose life and blessing every single day. Move her to choose Your instruction, knowledge, and wisdom instead of earthly riches and selfish gain (Proverbs 8:10).

Help my wife clearly see the way You would have her lead her life as an example to our children. May she boldly stand beside me and proclaim with me, "as for me and my household, we will serve the Lord" (Joshua 24:15). Help her rise above present circumstances and see with an eternal perspective so she can make decisions based on Your will. If she makes a choice not glorifying to You, nudge her conscience to repentance.

All of our own ways seem right to us, but You, oh Lord, weigh the heart (Proverbs 21:2). Weigh my wife's heart and remove any offensive way in her that might hinder the choices she makes throughout her day. Keep her mind unobstructed when she is faced with decisions. Show her where she may be trusting too much in her own thinking rather than depending on You for guidance. Help her clearly confirm and accept the ways You want her to go.

Lord, I pray you will protect my wife from unhealthy pressures and expectations of this world that could drive her to make choices that ruin her mind, body, and soul. Direct her heart to say "no" to unhealthy relationships, harmful business deals, corrupting thoughts, or selfish motivations. Supply her with wisdom so she may be kept in safety (Proverbs 28:26). In Jesus' precious name, Amen.

35

EVALUATING FRIENDSHIPS

He who walks with the wise grows wise, but a companion of fools suffers harm.

Proverbs 13:20

Proverbs 12:26
Proverbs 18:24
Proverbs 22:24-25
1 Corinthians 15:33-34

Dear Jesus, You are our one forever faithful Friend. You are the One Who sticks closer than a brother (Proverbs 18:24), but You did not intend us to walk this earth alone or without friends in human flesh and form. You have encouraged us to walk with the good and the upright so that we might not grow weary in doing good or grow weak and complacent in our faith. So, Father, today I pray my wife will seek out friends who are wise and gentle. Give her friends who, as iron sharpens iron, will sharpen her (Proverbs 27:17), and encourage her to keep on in the faith doing what is good, honorable, and respectable in Your name.

Help my wife be cautious in friendships (Proverbs 12:26), not choosing company that would lead her down a path that is evil (Proverbs 16:28-29). Give her wisdom to see where she may need to discontinue any friendship that is not uplifting to her character. Do not let her make friends with a hot-tempered or easily angered person, lest she learn to do the same (Proverbs 22:24-25). Give her the knowledge to know she needs to avoid anyone who talks too much, for such a person is prone to gossip and is not trustworthy (Proverbs 20:19).

Father, I pray my wife would be a woman who attracts godly friends. Remind her to listen before she speaks and walk in the humility it takes to put others before herself. Do not allow her to expect from others what she doesn't expect from herself. Encourage her to be a friend like Jesus; one of integrity, not easily swayed by the opinions or status of others (Mark 12:14), but treating each person with dignity and respect. In Jesus' name, Amen.

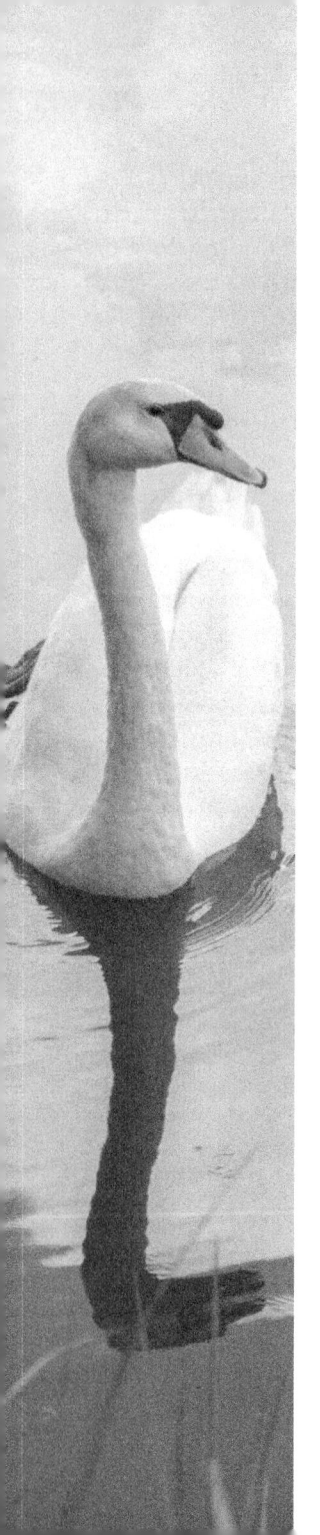

36

HEALTH OF BODY AND SOUL

Humility and the fear of the Lord bring wealth and honor and life.

Proverbs 22:4

Proverbs 3:7-8,
Romans 12:1
1 Corinthians 6:19-20
3 John 1:2

Father, You are the Healer who knows our bodies better than we do. Today, I pray that my wife's body will be kept in perfect harmony, working together and functioning the way You designed it to.

Father, help my wife take care of her body, for it is the temple where Your Spirit resides (1 Corinthians 3:16-17). I pray You would convict my wife to make healthy eating choices, not consuming anything that could harm or inhibit her from doing the work You have called her to do. Help her understand that she was bought at a price and she should honor You with her body (1 Corinthians 6:19-20). I pray she would not succumb to any food or substance addictions, but that in view of Your great mercy, offer her body as a living sacrifice, holy and pleasing to You (Romans 12:1).

Father, I pray also for my wife's spiritual health. Urge her to obedience to Your Word, growing her ever closer to You. Do not let her forget Your teaching, but help her store Your commands in her heart, so they may prolong her life and make her prosperous in all she does (Proverbs 3:1-2). Let her not be wise as the world considers wise. I pray she will seek first to fear You and shun evil for that will bring health to her body and nourishment to her bones (Proverbs 3:7-8). Give her wisdom and the knowledge to understand that her first and foremost duty on this earth is to obey You and glorify You (Ecclesiastes 12:13).

Father, I pray that my wife may enjoy good health and that all may go well with her, even as her soul continues growing well (3 John 1:2). Then, at the end of her long, obedient, and good life, I pray she may cross over into Your arms gently, easily, peacefully, and joyfully. In Jesus' name, Amen.

37

HEALTHY EMOTIONS

For the mind set on the flesh is death, but the mind set on the Spirit is life and peace.

Romans 8:6

Psalm 30:1-3
Psalm 31:3-5
Proverbs 16:32
Isaiah 61:3,7
Philippians 4:6-7

Father, I pray You would instruct my wife regarding her emotions. Help her feel and express her emotions in healthy ways. I pray You would demolish all strongholds, removing any diseases of the mind or unhealthy emotional behaviors like anger, depression, indifference, fear, hopelessness or suicidal thoughts. Deliver her from any negative ways of thinking. Help her not be anxious about anything, but in everything give thanks (Philippians 4:6-7). When she feels depressed or anxious, remind her to call upon Your name so that she may find peace and great joy in Your presence. Redeem her soul; spare her from sinking him into the pits of despair (Psalm 30:3).

When my wife is frustrated, give her the wisdom and strength to control her words and actions. Do not let her be controlled by anger or fits of rage. Instead, renew her to a gentle, understanding spirit. I pray she would not be a jealous or selfish woman who is always seeking but never finding, always wanting yet never content. Pour into her heart the emotions of thanksgiving and appreciation.

Father, free my wife from any shame she might have in sharing her true emotions. Where her emotions may not be processing in healthy ways, help her overcome. Lord, help me be a safe place for her to process her thoughts and feelings. Do not let me be insensitive to her when she needs to pour things out. Help me listen and not try to tell her how to fix things. Make me the steady listening ear she can confide in and the strong arms she can feel safe in.

Lord, I ask that You would bless my wife with a steadied heart, mind, and soul. Renew her, strengthen her, and empower her against any effects negative emotions bring. Instead of grief and sadness, anoint her with the oil of Your gladness. Instead of despair, give her a garment of praise Isaiah 61:3). Instead of shame, let her receive a double portion of rejoicing for her trials and heartbreaks (Isaiah 61:7). In Jesus' name, Amen.

38

OVERCOMING HABITS

...for a man is a slave to whatever has mastered him.

2 Peter 2:19

Psalm 19:13
Philippians 4:13
1 John 2:15-17

Father, You have sent Your Holy Spirit to live in us. Our bodies are a temple, a place for us to meet with You. I pray my wife will not let anything consume her body or mind that could destroy this temple, for You have said, those who destroy Your temple You will destroy also (1 Corinthians 3:16-17).

I pray my wife will not be addicted to any harmful food or substance, nor participate in drunkenness or gluttony. I pray she will not be tempted to sin against her body by using or participating in pornography, sexual immorality, orgies, or the like. Keep her mind pure. Do not let her fall into the habitual ways of thinking that come from jealousy, anger, witchcraft, idolatry, or dissensions. I stand on behalf of my wife and order away from her any tendency to gratify the flesh or seek self-satisfaction (Galatians 5:19-21). Do not let her be a woman mastered by sinful desires (2 Peter 2:19). Instead, establish in her a clean heart with pure motives matched with the strength to stand against the enemy's temptations.

I come before You, Lord, asking that You keep my wife from any willful sin. Do not let her be ruled by her flesh (Psalm 19:13). Surround her with Your mighty protection. Lift her when she stumbles; carry her when she is weak. Strengthen her when she is tempted and convict her to persevere in what she knows is good, always growing into a greater faith. Remind her to be careful how she lives - not as unwise but as wise, making the best choice in every situation (Ephesians 5:15). After she has persevered, Lord, may she praise You, knowing she can do all things through the power of Your love and grace. In Jesus' precious name, Amen.

39

VICTORY OVER HER PAST

Lord,
help me choose
forgiveness,
not dwelling on
the past,
but placing it
all at the
foot of the cross.

Amen.

Ecclesiastes 7:10
Philippians 3:13-15
Isaiah 43:18-19
2 Corinthians 4:16-18

Dear Jesus, thank You that You are able to set us free from all things past and present. You heal the broken-hearted and bind up their wounds (Proverbs 147:3). You have made a way for us to experience true freedom, and for that, I humbly thank You.

Bind up my wife's wounds, Jesus. Soothe her heart. Pour grace and mercy into her so that she may be able to forgive those who have hurt her. While it may be hard to forget what has been done to her, or what hasn't been done for her, I pray she would not lose heart but be strengthened day by day. Remind her that these troubles on earth are but momentary, helping her fix her eyes on You and cling tightly to Your great promises (2 Corinthians 4:16-18).

Father, You have told us to let go of former things and not dwell on the past (Isaiah 43:18-19). I pray my wife will not live in the past, nor let it dictate her in any way. Instead, heighten her ability to do better for those coming after her. Strengthen her to stand against any generational sins that may be holding onto her. Help my wife see that You have a great and wonderful plan for her and that You are calling her to set a new direction, a worthy heritage for her descendants.

Lord, help my wife understand that You are capable of renewing all things. That it is You who establishes a way through the desert and makes streams of life flow through wastelands of sin and pain. In Jesus' name, I stand against any powers and principalities of darkness that try to make her believe there is no hope. I lift my wife to You, trusting You to make her an over-comer. Though thousands would fall around her, in You she will remain unshaken.

Father, I pray that through my wife's complete deliverance, she would grow to find an appreciation for her past. May remembrances of her past serve only as reminders of Your great love and redeeming power, and result in praises to You for her healing and growth. May only peace, joy, thankfulness and greater faith come from the pain and heartbreak she has endured. Match and multiply the days of her gladness in proportion to her affliction (Psalm 90:15). In Jesus' name, Amen.

Prayers in Scripture

MOSES' PRAYER FOR DIRECTION AND FAVOR
Exodus 33:12-13

THE LORD'S PRAYER
Matthew 6:6-14

ASA'S PRAYER FOR VICTORY
2 Chronicles 14:11

**DAVID'S PRAYER FOR
HIS SON'S FAITHFULNESS**
1 Chronicles 29:16-19

PRAYER OF JABEZ
1 Chronicles 4:10

PAUL'S THANKSGIVING FOR GOD'S MERCY
1 Timothy 1:12-17

**THE BELIEVER'S PRAYER FOR
BOLDNESS IN CHRIST**
Acts 4:24-30

A PRAYER FOR SPIRITUAL CLEANSING
Psalm 51:1-12

A PRAYER FOR CHRIST-LIKE LOVE
Ephesians 3:14-21

A PRAYER TO SUCCEED IN THE LORD
Psalm 20:1-9

40

HOPE FOR YOUR FUTURE

Whether it is
favorable or
unfavorable,
we will obey
the Lord our God...
so that it may
go well with us...

Jeremiah 42:6

Psalm 16:8
Psalm 25:4-5
Psalm 26:2-3
Psalm 27:4-5

Father, thank You for this woman You have set in my life. I pray You will give her a clear vision of what Your plan is for her. I pray that she will not pursue things of her own will but seek You first in all things, so she may lead her life in ways that are good, right, and beneficial to our marriage and our home.

Instruct her, Lord, in the way You would have her go. Stay at her right hand so she will not be shaken (Psalm 16:7). You have promised to give to each person that which they have done. I pray my wife will be a woman who persistently seeks You in all she does and wherever she goes so that she may inherit eternal life (Romans 2:6-7).

Father, surround my wife and me with Your mighty wings. Illuminate the path You would have us walk together, while still remaining obedient to the individual call You have on each of our lives. Strengthen us so that we may march courageously onward in obedience, whether the storm is favorable or unfavorable. I pray we would always be careful to live uprightly and act wisely, never letting an opportunity to bring glory to You go to waste (Ephesians 5:15-16). Lead us in ways that are right so that all may go well with us, our marriage, and our descendants. In Jesus' precious name, Amen.

ABCs OF CHRISTIAN MARRIAGE

A marriage steeped in connection and trust is one of the most beautiful things on earth. So much so, that most of us would say there is no meaning, purpose or value in life if we don't have someone to share love, fears, failures and successes with; someone to know and be known by.

Someone to laugh with, cry with, love. The one we do life with. The one we still choose after we've experienced their worst. The one who still chooses us when we've demonstrated our failures.

Using the alphabet as a guide, we find words or phrases that encourage us to contribute value, meaning, and commitment to our marriage. Many of these are drawn from Bible verses, others are implied or just good old common sense. Enjoy!

ATTITUDE ADJUSTMENT

"Your attitude should be the same as that of Christ Jesus."

Philippians 2:5

To find a better understanding of what kind of attitude that is, you might consider reading Philippians 2:3-8.

BUILD EACH OTHER

"Let us therefore make every effort to do
what leads to peace and mutual edification."

Romans 14:19

"[E]ncourage one another daily, as long as it is called Today, so that none of you may be hardened by sin's deceitfulness."

Hebrews 3:13

"Therefore encourage one another and build each other up."

1 Thessalonians 5:11

CONTENT

"Do not say, "Why were the old days better than these?" For it is not wise to ask such questions."

Ecclesiastes 7:10

"[B]e content with what you have, because God has said, "Never will I leave you; never will I forsake you.""

Hebrews 13:5

DONATE YOUR EARS

"Everyone should be quick to listen, slow to speak and slow to become angry."

James 1:19

EJECT ANGER

"Get rid of all bitterness, rage and anger, brawling and slander, along with every form of malice."

Ephesians 4:31

FORFEIT GRUDGES

"Do not repay anyone evil for evil...Do not take revenge, my friends, but leave room for God's wrath, for it is written: "It is mine to avenge; I will repay," says the Lord."

Romans 12:17,19

"A heart at peace gives life to the body, but envy rots the bones."

Proverbs 14:30

GENTLENESS & KINDNESS

"Let your gentleness be known to all."

Philippians 4:5

"Be kind and compassionate to one another, forgiving each other, just as in Christ God forgave you."

Ephesians 4:32

HELP EACH OTHER

"Two are better than one, because they have a good return for their work: If one falls down, his friend can help him up."

Ecclesiastes 4:9-10

INDUCE LOVE

"Be imitators of God, therefore, as dearly beloved children and live a life of love, just as Christ loved us and gave Himself up for us as a fragrant offering and sacrifice to God."

Ephesians 5:1-2

"Let no debt remain outstanding, except the continuing debt to love one another, for he who loves his fellowman has fulfilled the law. The commandments...are summed up in this one rule: "Love your neighbor as yourself." Love does no harm to its neighbor. Therefore love is the fulfillment of the law."

Romans 13:8-10

JOY TO ONE ANOTHER

"You have stolen my heart, my sister, my bride;
you have stolen my heart with one glance of your eyes...
How delightful is your love, my sister, my bride!
How much more pleasing is your love than wine."

Song of Solomon 4:9-10

"He seldom reflects on the days of his life,
because God keeps him occupied with gladness of heart."

Ecclesiastes 5:20

"Enjoy life with your wife (spouse), whom you love."

Ecclesiastes 9:9

KISS PASSIONATELY

"Let him kiss me with the kisses of his mouth—
for your love is more delightful than wine."

Song of Solomon 1:2

"Your lips drop sweetness as the honeycomb, my bride;
milk and honey are under your tongue."

Song of Solomon 4:11

LEAD YOURSELF WELL

In short, be responsible for yourself. You control your actions, your words, all of you. Do it well and do it first.

"Do not think of yourself more highly than you ought,
but rather think of yourself with sober judgment."

Romans 12:3

MAKE UP

"If anyone has caused grief...you ought to forgive and comfort him, so that he will not be overwhelmed by excessive sorrow. I urge you, therefore, to reaffirm your love for him."

2 Corinthians 2:5-8

NOTICE EACH OTHERS NEEDS

"If anyone does not provide for his relatives, and especially for his immediate family, he has denied the faith and is worse than an unbeliever."

1 Timothy 5:8

ORGANIZE PRIORITIES

"But seek first His kingdom and his righteousness, and all these things will be given to you as well."

Matthew 6:33

"So we make it our goal to please Him, whether we are at home in the body or away from it."

2 Corinthians 5:9

PRAY

"And pray in the Spirit on all occasions with all kinds of
prayers and requests. With this in mind,
be alert and always keep on praying."

Ephesians 6:18

QUIET ARGUMENTS before they start

"A gentle answer turns away wrath,
but a harsh word stirs up anger."

Proverbs 15:1

"A hot-tempered man stirs up dissension,
but a patient man calms a quarrel."

Proverbs 15:18

R-RATED IS GOOD

Song of Solomon. That's all for this one!

SERVE EACH OTHER

"[S]erve one another in love. The entire law is summed up in
one single command: "Love your neighbor as yourself."

Galatians 5:13-14

THANKFUL FOR EACH OTHER

"I thank my God every time I remember you."

Philippians 1:3

UNDERSTANDING TOWARD EACH OTHER

"A patient man has great understanding."

Proverbs 14:29

"Love is patient...It always protects, always trusts, always hopes, always perseveres. Love never fails."

1 Corinthians 13:4-8

VERBALIZE FEELINGS APPROPRIATELY

Throwing around accusations that begin with "You always..." or, "You never..." is hardly beneficial to your spouse. It feels more like an attack. Telling your spouse how they've hurt you needs to be done kindly and calmly to avoid causing more pain.

"A man of knowledge uses words with restraint, and a man of understanding is even-tempered."

Proverbs 17:27

"Reckless words pierce like a sword,
but the tongue of the wise brings healing."

Proverbs 12:18

WISE WORDS

"The heart of the righteous weighs its answers,
but the mouth of the wicked gushes evil."

Proverbs 15:28

"She speaks with wisdom and
faithful instruction is on her tongue."

Proverbs 31:26

eXTEND GRACE

"He who loves a pure heart and whose speech is gracious
will have the king for his friend."

Proverbs 22:11

"A fool shows his annoyance at once,
but a prudent man overlooks an insult."

Proverbs 12:16

"A kindhearted woman gains respect."

Proverbs 11:16

YIELD YOUR RIGHT TO BE RIGHT

"Be completely humble and gentle;
be patient, bearing with one another in love.
Make every effort to keep the unity of the Spirit
through the bond of peace."

Ephesians 4:2-3

ZEALOUS FOR A LIFE TOGETHER

"Whether it is favorable or unfavorable,
we will obey the Lord our God...
so that it will go well with us,
for we will obey the Lord our God."

Jeremiah 42:6

kayleneyoder.com

More from Kaylene Yoder

40 Scripture-Based Prayers
to Pray Over Your Husband

40 Scripture-Based Prayers
to Pray Over Your Children

A Wife's 40-Day Fasting & Prayer Journal
(devotional)

ABC Scripture Cards
for the Christian Marriage

Prayer Cards for
Husbands, Wives, and Parents

Prayer Challenges

R.E.S.T. Bible Study Method and Journals

and free printable resources can be found at:

https://kayleneyoder.com

Made in the USA
Columbia, SC
19 February 2020